i

Printed in the United States of America

Baird Farms Publishing Company LLC
Mount Juliet, TN 37122

First Edition

10987654321

ISBN 978-1-945450-10-5

Copyright ©2020 JoAnn A. Quitmeyer

All rights reserved. This book may not be copied or reproduced in part or in whole, unless for review or promotional purposes, without the written consent of the Publisher.

This book is dedicated to the memory of my husband,
Wallace D. Quitmeyer.

I LOVE TRAINS!
by J. A. Quitmeyer

On display at Cheekwood Botanical Gardens in Nashville, TN during the summer of 2011, an outdoor train exhibit was designed by Paul Busse of Alexandria, KY.

Photographs were taken of this one-of-a-kind exhibit by Wallace D. Quitmeyer of Hermitage, TN. Included were seven garden scale trains running on 1000 feet of track, through tunnels and over bridges as they passed by historic Tennessee landmarks. The landscape included 2500 tiny trees, shrubs, ground covers and flowering plants.

Tennessee landmarks include Ryman Auditorium, Graceland, Cades Cove Cabin, Belle Meade Plantation, Alex Haley House, Old York Mill, the Parthenon, Union Station and the Tennessee State Capital.

This story is written to correspond with these photographs and is dedicated to the memory of Wallace. D. Quitmeyer.

Some trains go up,

Some trains go down,

Some trains just seem

To go 'round and 'round.

Through valleys and towns,

The trains will go;

In rain or snow

Their whistles blow.

Trains roar by

Up in the air,

A very fast way

To get somewhere.

Pulled by a powerful

Engine or two,

Some rows of cars

Carry people like you.

One car follows

Right after the other.

It's hard to tell

One from another.

A train may travel

A scenic route;

If on a commuter,

It takes you to work.

Riding a train

Is sure to thrill,

As a new experience

Or a way up the hill.

Some trains are loaded

With coal and ore,

And tractors and cars,

They haul everywhere.

Flat cars, box cars,
And open hopper bins,
All kinds of cars
That hold many things.

A train is a fast
And efficient way
To move all the things
We use every day.

And what a surprise!
Some trains we see,
Have engines that
Sort of look like me.

With big bright eyes
And a happy smile,
These trains keep chugging
Mile after mile.

These happy cars
Are loved by all,
From aging folks
To babies that crawl.

Tennessee State House
Nashville, TN

As we go traveling

Down the track,

We see many places

We would like to go back.

There is the State House

Where laws are made.

You must obey or

Your freedom will fade.

Graceland
Memphis, TN

Graceland was home

Of the great singer, Elvis.

He really knew how

To shake his pelvis.

And there is the Ryman,

Home of the Opry!

Stars may be heard

As they sing "Country".

Ryman Auditorium
Nashville, TN

The Parthenon,
Nashville, TN

Is that the Parthenon

That I see?

Inside is Athena

And a painting or three.

Union Station was once

A place trains would linger.

Now, inside, you can

Satisfy your hunger.

Union Station
Nashville, TN

See old structures

Of days long past.

The lifestyle is gone

But the buildings last.

Carter House

Cheekwood Mansion

Nashville, TN

The Alex Haley House
And the Old York Mill,
Rocky Mount and
Marble Spring by the hill.

Alex Haley House

Old York Mill

Rocky Mount 1770

Marble Spring

Belle Meade Plantation
Is now open;
See Casey Jones' House
And Cades Cove Cabin

Belle Meade Mansion, Nashville, TN

Casey Jones House

Cadis Cove Cabin

Way up on bridges
Soaring so high,
As we watch the trains,
We think they can fly.

Look up as the tracks
Climb to the sky.
Can we touch that star?
It seems right nearby!

Up on the mountain

And down by the stream,

This beautiful scene makes it

Seem like a dream.

Some trains are big,

Some trains are small;

It doesn't matter,

I love them all.

If you stand and watch

You, too, will see,

As the trains go by,

You love them like me.

I LOVE TRAINS!

About the Author

JoAnn Quitmeyer has written and illustrated children's books under the pen name of E. Emma Zimmer and published by Same Old Story Publishing. *Annabelle Anteater's First Day of School* and *Purple* written by Joseph Hornesby and illustrated by J. A. Quitmeyer have been released by Same Old Story Publishing Co. and soon will be reissued by Baird Farms Publishing Company edited by J.A. Quitmeyer.

Ms. Quitmeyer has authored over 150 peer-reviewed articles on industrial cleaning and corrosion issues published in numerous professional journals. She has also authored two text books and numerous chapters published on chemistry and industrial cleaning, most recently in *Handbook of Industrial Cleaning, Volume I,* published by CRC Press and *Modern Industrial Cleaning, With Health, Safety and the Environment in Mind* published by Same Old Story Publishing Co.

She spent her career as a chemist, formulating cleaning, lubrication and corrosion inhibiting products for EcoLab Corp. in St. Paul, MN and W. R. Grace, Lexington, MA and retired as Director of Research and Development at Kyzen Corporation in Nashville, TN. She now is the editor and publisher for Baird Farms Publishing Company located in Mt. Juliet, TN.

Acknowledgements

A big thank you goes to my husband of 50 years, the late Wallace D. Quitmeyer, for taking all the photographs included in this book. I also would like to thank Cheekwood and Paul Busse for creating this garden train exhibit at Cheekwood Botanical Gardens in Nashville, TN.

www.ingramcontent.com/pod-product-compliance
Lightning Source LLC
Chambersburg PA
CBHW041504220426
43661CB00016B/1248